For _____

The Polish Housewife Cookbook

Traditional recipes you wish
your babcia (Polish grandmother) had written down

Lois Britton

Lois Britton

8 November 2019

For more information, please contact Lois Britton at lois@polishhousewife.com.

ISBN 978-0-578-57384-7

Book design by Jeanine Colini Design Art (jcda.com)
Photography by Lois Britton

To my parents, Jim and Jeanne,
who let me play in the kitchen
at an early age and
always made me feel that
anything was possible.

to Ed, who provided the adventure,
unending support,
and encouragement;

to Elżbieta, Gosia, Klaudia, Sławek,
Szymon, Angelika, Grzegorz, Maria,
Zbigniew, and Ewa & Norbert,
who have all let me follow them
into the kitchen.

Introduction

The connection between family and food is so strong. Think about meals with extended family. Multiple generations in the kitchen cooking together. The special feeling of holiday gatherings. I hope this cookbook will be connected to your future memories.

For the reader who is well versed in Polish cuisine, I'm grateful and honored that you're adding this book to your collection. For the reader who has fond memories of Polish cooking but didn't get the recipes, because no matter what the heritage, grandmothers are well known for keeping recipes in their heads—or have simply gotten out of the habit of preparing childhood favorites—it warms my heart to reconnect you with your culinary heritage. After all, food is my love language.

Maybe you're someone like me, who doesn't have a Polish heritage, but has a spirit of culinary adventure and an appreciation for good food from around the globe. I'm thrilled to share what I have found in Poland with you.

In a book devoted to Polish recipes, I must share some thoughts on Polish hospitality. An invitation to a Polish home is a special occasion. Invitations are not made lightly. Receiving an invitation is a sign that your relationship is considered important.

As a guest, you will be overwhelmed by the hospitality. Your hosts will make every effort to share their very best with you. You can expect a variety of dishes and will be offered second and third helpings. The meal could easily go on for hours at a lovely, leisurely pace with lots of conversation, ending with a homemade fruit liqueur. It's an experience to treasure.

Polish people really know good food. And you don't have to visit a posh restaurant to find it. Whether it's a stop at a roadside country inn, or at a simple neighborhood coffee shop, both will deliver food that's well worth remembering.

That is what I hope you will find here: food that is well worth remembering. For some time now, readers have been asking if I have a cookbook, saying that it would be nice to have all my recipes in one place. I am very happy that the time has arrived for this volume.

I've selected traditional Polish recipes, perennial favorites—classics, so to speak. Some have been published on my website; some have been newly photographed; and some are new for me. I hope you will enjoy them all, prepare them often, and share them with your extended family and friends.

You might want to buy a dill plant. You'll use it frequently. And you might like to add some whole allspice and ground marjoram to your spice cabinet.

Cooks like to put their own spin on things. You might find an ingredient in a recipe that your family never used. Please know that for some recipes, there are as many variations as there are kitchens in Poland. The recipes I offer are a starting point—and you should feel free to make them your own.

It often surprises people that I'm not Polish. Nor is my husband, Ed. He had the advantage of growing up with lots of Polish kids near Pittsburgh, Pennsylvania. I, on the other hand, had no exposure to Polish food or culture until Ed started working in Poland. I was a new food blogger at the time, and when I joined him in Poznań, I made it my mission to learn all that I could about Polish cooking. That continues to this day. It makes me so happy to hear from my readers that my new discoveries have reconnected them with their past.

Polish pronunciation

Readers often ask for the proper pronunciation of Polish recipe titles. I'll offer the following very basic guide to help you in sounding out Polish words. The accent is always on the next to last syllable, and when in doubt, you can always type a word in Google translate and click on the speaker icon to hear the word pronounced. It's not perfect, but it helps.

The following are pronounced as they are in English:
b d f h k l m n p t z

a – like the a in ball

c – like the ts in cats

e – like the e in bet

g – like the g in grab

i – like the ee in feel

j – like the y in yes

o – like the o in order

r – roll your Rs

s – like the s in silly

u – like the oo in moose

w – like a v

y – like the y in myth

ą – a nasal o, like on or om

ć, ci – a soft tch

ę – a nasal e, like en or em

ł – like an English w

ń, ni – like the Spanish ñ

ó – the same as a Polish u, like oo

ś, si – a soft sh

ź, zi – a soft zh

ż – like the zh in Zhivago

ch – like an h

cz – like the ch in chip

dz – like the ds in lads

dź, dzi – like the g in gene

dż – like the j in John

rz – a hard zh, like ż

sz – like the sh in shore

Contents

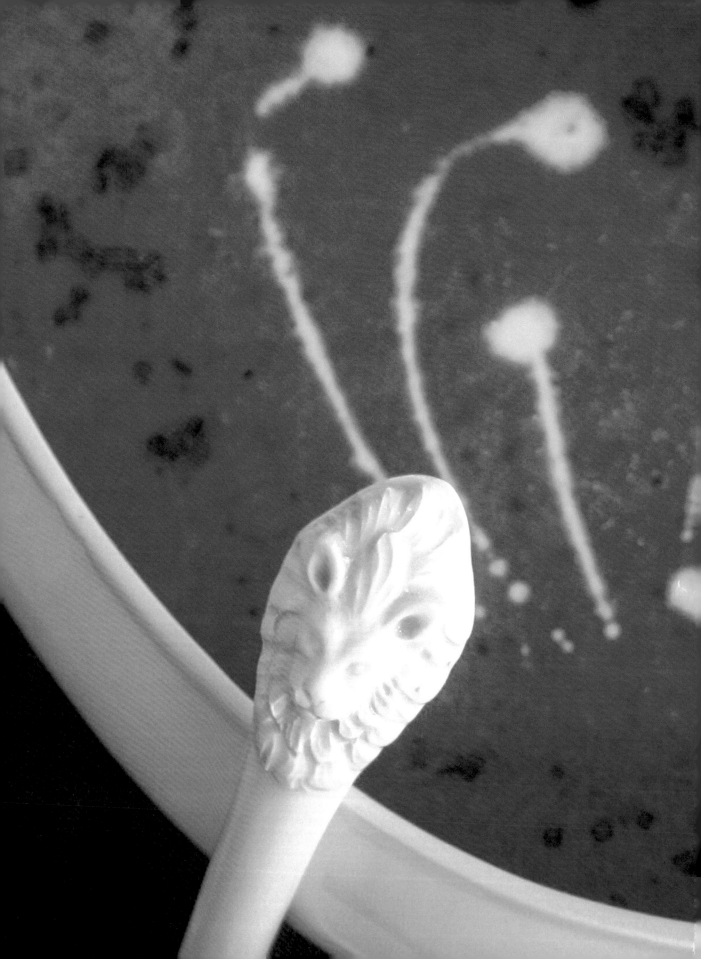

Soups | Zupy

Soup is the most popular first course in Poland, and soup is something most Poles know how to make from scratch and regularly do. Grocers have made it convenient and inexpensive to make soup. You can buy a chicken torso (without breasts, wings, thighs or legs to make chicken broth.

There is the same convenience in the produce section. Every market whether they're a neighborhood convenience store or a chain supermarket will sell a package of veggies for soup making. They usually include a few carrots, a parsnip, a leek, a slice of celery root, a sprig of flat-leaf parsley, and sometimes, a cross-section slice of savoy cabbage. You'll see this combination of vegetables used repeatedly in these recipes. For about $3.00, you have everything you need to make a good pot of soup without buying large quantities that might go to waste.

Chilled creamy beet soup | Chłodnik

Potato soup | Zupa ziemniaczana

Chicken noodle soup |Rosół

Dill pickle soup | Zupa ogórkowa

Cauliflower soup | Zupa kalafiorowa

Spicy beet broth | Barszcz

Tripe soup | Flaki

Sour rye soup | Żurek

Sauerkraut soup | Kapuśniak

Tomato soup | Zupa pomidorowa

Chilled creamy beet soup
Chłodnik

Originally a Lithuanian recipe, Chłodnik has become a summer classic in Poland – something I think of as Polish gazpacho. You'll find it on every menu and in the family fridge. I learned this recipe from my friend Gosia who taught me and two other friends from our international book club. When her teenage son came downstairs to join us, he was delighted to see the big pot of soup – pleased that he could have some for his breakfast the next day too.

Ingredients

4 or 5 young, tender beets with tops

1/2 teaspoon salt

2 cucumbers

6 radishes, grated

3 tablespoons fresh dill, chopped

2 green onions, chopped

4 cups plain yogurt

4 cups plain kefir or buttermilk

1 cup sour cream

salt and pepper, to taste

3 hard-boiled eggs, peeled and quartered

Prep time: 30 minutes
Cook time: 15 minutes
Servings: 10-12

Instructions

1. Prepare the beets by removing and dicing the stems up to the leaves. Add the chopped stems to a large soup pot. Peel and shred the beetroots, add to the pan with enough water just to cover the beets. Add salt and simmer until tender, about 15 minutes. Cool.

2. While the beets are cooking, peel and shred the cucumbers and grate the radishes. After the beets have cooled, add the cucumbers and radishes to the pan along with dill, green onions, yogurt, kefir, and sour cream; season with salt and pepper.

3. Chill and serve garnished with a hard-boiled egg

Potato soup
Zupa ziemniaczana

As a child, my family often had potato soup for supper, served with buttered saltine crackers. It was a meal that I always looked forward to. This soup is heartier than the potato soup I knew way back when, with more veggies and a little meat. The smooth, tasty layers of flavor make this a favorite for young and old(er) alike.

Ingredients

8 strips of bacon, divided

4 ounces of Polish sausage

1 large onion, diced

1 large carrot, diced

1 parsnip, diced

1 stalk of celery, diced

2 pounds of potatoes (2 large Russets)

8 cups chicken broth

2 bay leaves

4 allspice berries

Salt & pepper, to taste

2 tablespoons Wondra* flour

1 cup sour cream

1 teaspoon ground marjoram

Wondra is flour that has already been cooked, so there is no raw flour taste and it blends in easily to thicken soups and gravies.

Prep time: 20 minutes
Cook time: 55 minutes
Servings: 6-8 servings

Instructions

1. Cut the bacon into ½ inch pieces. Quarter the Polish sausage lengthwise and cut into ½ inch pieces. Peel and cube the potatoes. In a Dutch oven, sauté the bacon until crisp, remove from the pan and reserve half for topping.

2. Cook the Polish sausage in the bacon grease until it just begins to brown and remove from the pan. Cook onion, carrot, parsnip, and celery until onion is translucent. Return half of the bacon, and all the sausage to the pan. Add potatoes, broth, bay leaves, allspice, salt, and pepper. Go easy on the salt, the meats and stock will add salt too.

3. Bring to a boil and simmer until vegetables are tender, about 20 minutes. Lightly sprinkle Wondra flour and stir into soup. Add small amounts at a time to avoid clumping. Add marjoram (you'll get the most flavor adding this at the end of the cooking time) and serve.

Chicken soup
Rosół

We first sampled Rosół on an icy cold Saturday. We'd stopped by a favorite restaurant in the Stary Rynek for lunch. The waiter knew I was new in Poland and explained to me that this soup was traditional for Sunday dinner. He said the nice thing was you could stretch one chicken to feed the entire extended family because you never know who might drop by.

Ingredients

5-pound chicken, whole or bone-in pieces

1 beef soup bone

3 turkey necks

2 large onions

5 carrots, trimmed and peeled

2 parsnips, trimmed and peeled

1 leek, trimmed, use the white and light green part

1 small-to-medium celery root peeled, or 3 stalks celery

1/4 small savoy cabbage

1 whole clove

4 allspice berries

2 bay leaves

4 sprigs fresh flat-leaf parsley

4 sprigs fresh dill (optional) plus some for garnish

6 peppercorns

1 tablespoon salt (adjust the amount to taste)

thin noodles (optional)

Prep time: 20 minutes
Cook time: 2 1/2 hours
Servings: 8 servings

Instructions

1. Add chicken, beef bone, and turkey necks to a large Dutch oven or stockpot, cover with water and bring to a boil. Simmer for 2 to 2 1/2 hours, skimming any impurities off the top to ensure a clear broth.

2. Trim the root end of the onions and cut in half (leave the yellow skin on, it adds great color). If your pot is big enough, add the vegetables and spices for the last hour of the cooking time. My Dutch oven wasn't big enough to hold everything, just the chicken and other bones filled the pot, so I cooked the meat/bones for the full cooking time, then removed them, and cooked the vegetables and spices in the broth.

3. Place a colander over a large bowl or pan, and pour the soup into the colander. Return the broth you just strained to the original pan.

4. Bone the chicken, pulling the meat into large chunks, slice the carrots, return the chicken and carrots to the broth.

5. If using noodles, cook according to package instructions. Add noodles to a bowl and then top with hot soup. This keeps the noodles from swelling up with broth and keeps the broth clear.

Sour pickle soup
Zupa ogórkowa

When I made my first batch of brined pickles, an American friend who has lived in Wrocław for years said, "Now, you need to make ogórkowa." So I did. The sour pickles meld beautifully with the other ingredients. It's milder than you might expect for a pickle soup!

Ingredients

Pork or chicken bones

1 leek, the white and light green parts, trimmed and rinsed

2 carrots, trimmed and peeled

1 parsnip, trimmed and peeled

1 stalk celery, trimmed

1 onion, trimmed and outer layer removed

3 allspice (whole)

1 quart (900 ml) sour pickles

4 cloves garlic, finely minced

3 large potatoes, peeled and diced

1 tablespoon dried marjoram

salt and pepper, to taste

1/4 cup heavy cream

2 tablespoons chopped fresh dill

Prep time: 15 minutes
Cook time: 1 hour
Servings: 6-8 servings

Instructions

1. Add the bones, leek, carrots, parsnip, celery, onion and allspice to a large pot. Add 6 to 8 cups of water. If you don't have soup bones on hand, you can use chicken or vegetable broth. Bring to a boil, reduce heat and simmer 40 minutes.

2. While this is cooking, remove the pickles, reserving their liquid. Grate the pickles and simmer in a small amount of water for 20 minutes, drain.

3. Add the garlic and potatoes to the soup and cook about 15 minutes, until the potatoes are tender. Remove the bones, leek, carrots, parsnip, onion, and allspice from the soup. Grate the carrots, parsnip, and celery, and return to the soup. Season with marjoram, salt, and pepper. Add the grated pickles and the reserved pickle juice to the soup. Just before serving, stir in the heavy cream and the dill.

Cauliflower soup
Zupa kalafiorowa

A wonderfully mild soup that is quick to prepare and easy to make vegetarian.

Ingredients

1 head cauliflower, cut into florets

2 carrots, peeled and diced

4 potatoes, peeled and finely diced

6 cups chicken or vegetable broth

1 egg yolk

1/2 cup heavy cream

salt and pepper, to taste

2 tablespoons chopped dill
and/or parsley

Prep time: 20 minutes
Cook time: 20 minutes
Servings: 8 servings

Directions

1. Add cauliflower, carrots, potatoes, and broth to a Dutch oven. Bring to a boil, reduce heat and simmer for about 20 minutes, until the vegetables are tender.

2. Beat yolk and cream, temper by slowly adding a ladle or two of hot broth, stirring constantly. Add to the soup.

3. Season with salt and pepper, and garnish with dill and/or parsley.

Spicy beet broth
Barszcz

With such a variety of veggies, you're guaranteed complex layers of flavor in this red beet broth, and with 10 cloves, garlic plays a predominant role. The sweetness of the beets is counterbalanced by the tartness of the lemon juice. Barszcz is often served with uszka, specially shaped pierogi filled with mushrooms and sauerkraut (p. 62-63), or krokietky which you'll find on my website at bit.ly/krokiet.

Ingredients

4 large or 6 small beets, peeled and halved

1-pound meaty beef bones

1 medium carrot, trimmed and peeled

1 medium parsnip, trimmed and peeled

1 large onion, peeled and halved

1 leek, white and green parts, trimmed, halved lengthwise and rinsed

1 long celery stalk

3-4 dried mushrooms

10 cloves garlic, peeled but left whole

1 bay leaf

1 large pinch of dried marjoram

6 peppercorns

about 12 cups of water, depending on the size of your pot

juice of 1 lemon, or about 4 tablespoons

salt and pepper

Prep time: 20 minutes
Cook time: 2 hours
Servings: 8 servings

Instructions

1. Add the beets, beef bones, carrot, parsnip, onion, leek, celery, mushrooms, garlic, bay leaf, marjoram, and peppercorns to a Dutch oven or stockpot. Add enough water to the pot to cover the ingredients. Bring to a boil, reduce heat and simmer for about two hours. Skim off foam as it appears.

2. Strain the soup through a colander. If it tastes watery, cook it down a bit to concentrate the flavors. Add lemon juice and season to taste with salt and pepper, it should taste garlicky and tart. I have added garlic powder at this point if the 10 cloves of garlic weren't strong enough. Do the same by adding more lemon juice or a bit of vinegar (a spoon at a time, tasting with each addition) to be sure the soup is pleasantly tart.

3. Serve the clear, hot soup in bowls or cups for sipping.

Tripe soup
Flaki

Flaki is loved by those who grew up with it. Those who didn't often pass it by because of the texture of the tripe or maybe just the thought of the tripe. The soup has a wonderful flavor and is rumored to cure a hangover.

Ingredients

3 pounds of honeycomb tripe

2 pounds beef soup bones

3 carrots, diced

2 large onions, diced

2 stalks celery, diced

10 whole allspice

10 black peppercorns

3 bay leaves

1 tablespoon hot paprika

1 tablespoon sweet paprika

1 tablespoon chopped fresh parsley

1 teaspoon dried marjoram

6 ounces tomato paste

salt & pepper, to taste

Prep time: 30 minutes
Cook time: 4 hours
Servings: 8-10 servings

Instructions

1. The tripe I purchased was perfectly clean, but if yours needs cleaning, use salt to give it a good scrubbing, then rinse. Put the tripe into a Dutch oven and cover with water, simmer until tender (about 3 hours).

2. Drain, discarding liquid and thinly slice the tripe into thin strips. Return to Dutch oven and add remaining ingredients, cover with water. Bring to a boil and simmer for about an hour.

3. Remove soup bones, picking off any meat and add the meat to the soup before serving.

Sour rye soup
Żurek

The first thing I must tell you, is that you'll need to prepare the sour liquid for the soup in advance. Allow five days! In a pinch, you could sour the broth with vinegar or sour cream, but it's worth doing properly if you can. Żurek, and its cousin White Barszcz, prepared with soured wheat flour rather than rye, are the most uniquely Polish dishes I've come across.

Ingredients

For zakwas (the sour liquid)

5 tablespoons rye flour

crust from a slice of rye bread (optional)

3 cups water

4 cloves garlic, crushed

3 bay leaves

5 allspice berries

For the soup

4 slices bacon, diced

1 pound Polish sausage, sliced

2 large onions, coarsely chopped

1 large carrot, sliced

1 large parsnip, sliced

1/2 celery root, peeled and diced

6 - 8 cups water

1 bay leaf

2 cloves crushed garlic

4 large potatoes, peeled and diced

1/2 teaspoon marjoram

salt & pepper, to taste

2 tablespoon horseradish (freshly grated or jarred)

2 tablespoons cream

hard-boiled eggs

Prep time: 5 days
Cook time: 50 minutes
Servings: 8 servings

Instructions

For the zakwas (the sour liquid)

1. Add the flour and crust (if you're using it) to a large jar. Add the water, garlic, bay leaves, and allspice and mix thoroughly. As it sits, it will separate with the flour sinking to the bottom. Cover the jar with a paper towel or kitchen towel (I like to secure it with a large rubber band). Let sit for five days, giving it a swirl daily to mix.

For the soup

2. Brown the bacon and sausage in a Dutch oven. Add the onion, carrot, parsnip, celery root, water, bay leaf, and garlic, simmer for 40 minutes.

3. Add the potatoes and marjoram, cook until the potatoes are tender. Add 2 cups of the zakwas (strained or flour mixed in, your choice). If you want the soup sourer, add the remaining zakwas.

4. Season with salt and pepper. Add horseradish and cream. Return to a boil and remove from heat. Serve by garnishing with hardboiled egg, halved or quartered.

Sauerkraut soup
Kapuśniak

There are a few notes to accompany the ingredients for this recipe. If you're using canned sauerkraut that has been soured with vinegar, you should rinse and drain the kraut. If your sauerkraut is naturally fermented, soured by lacto-fermentation, then just drain. The tartness of the latter is milder.

You can substitute pork neckbones for the spareribs. It's a variation many people have mentioned to me. Many have also said their family didn't use sugar. I forgot and left the sugar out one time, and I really missed it. It's especially important if you're using canned sauerkraut. The caramelized sugar doesn't make it sweet, but it adds to and enhances the soup flavor. It seems to make it less acidic, rounding out the flavor.

Ingredients

1 pound sauerkraut

4 cups beef broth or 4 cups water
   and 2 Knorr beef bouillon cubes

2 pounds pork spareribs

2 bay leaves

8 peppercorns

2 medium carrots, diced

2 ounces dried mushrooms
   (optional)

2 tablespoons sugar

Prep time: 30 minutes
Cook time: 2 hours
Servings: 6 servings

Directions

1. Rinse and drain the sauerkraut. In a large pot, add the broth, spareribs, bay leaves, peppercorns, carrots, and dried mushrooms. (Fresh chanterelles were in the market, so I sliced 2 cups instead. I think this was also easier than retrieving the dried, cooked mushrooms for slicing).

2. Simmer over low heat, uncovered, for 1 1/2 hours.

3. Remove the mushrooms and cut them into strips. Return them to the pot and add 4 more cups of water.

4. Melt the sugar over medium heat until it colors and caramelizes. Add the sauerkraut and the caramelized sugar to the pot, cover and cook for 30 minutes. Remove the ribs from the pot, pull the meat off the bones and slice into bite-sized strips; return to soup.

Tomato soup
Zupa pomidorowa

Beautiful color and complex flavor make this colorful dish a memorable first course.

Ingredients

3 14-ounce cans of tomatoes

3/4 cup olive oil, divided

salt and pepper, to taste

1 onion or leek (white and light green parts only), diced

1 carrot, diced

1 stalk celery or ½ cup celery root, diced

1 parsnip, diced (optional)

2 - 4 tablespoons brandy (or sherry)

2 tablespoons basil or parsley, chopped

1 cup chicken or vegetable stock

1/2 - 1 cup heavy cream

Prep time: 15 minutes
Cook time: 1 hour
Servings: 6 servings

Instructions

1. Preheat oven to 400° F.

2. Drain the tomatoes, reserving liquid, using your hands, open the tomatoes, removing the seeds. Lay the tomatoes out flat on a parchment-lined baking sheet, drizzle with 1/4 cup olive oil, sprinkle with salt and pepper, bake until edges begin to brown, about 20 minutes (if you use fire-roasted tomatoes, you can skip this step).

3. Add 1/2 cup olive oil to a large saucepan, add tomatoes, onion, carrot, celery, and parsnip. Cook over medium heat for 10 minutes. Add brandy and flame (you may not have enough alcohol to get a flame with sherry).

4. Add the herbs, reserved tomato juice, and the stock. Simmer until the veggies are tender. Process the soup using an immersion blender, blender, or food processor (you may want to let it cool a little bit, so you don't get splashed with hot soup). Add cream, using enough to get the desired texture, and heat until steaming. Garnish with a bit of cream and/or herbs.

Breads | Pieczywo

The bread is Poland is amazing! No matter where you buy it – bakery, budget supermarket or high end – it would all be called artisan bread if sold in the United States. Polish bread is amazingly fresh and is made without preservatives.

This section offers a variety of breads for you: from a crusty roll (the staple of college students on the run), to several loaves of bread that would be perfect for wiping up that last bit of Bigos (page 64-65) from your plate, and even a blueberry bun which would be ideal for dessert or with a cup of tea for second breakfast.

Bread rolls | Bułki

Sourdough rye | Chleb żytni razowy na zakwasie

Rye-Onion bread | Chleb żytni z cebulą

Blueberry bun | Jagodzianki

Krakow pretzel | Obwarzanek krakowski

White bread | Chleb pszenny

Potato bread | Chleb ziemniaczany

Braided egg bread | Chałka

Bread rolls
Bułki

Bułki are a Polish classic. You find them served with kiełbasa at soccer matches, and they're a staple for college students who get by with a roll and yogurt.

Use them to make a sandwich with cold cuts and cheese or use them to sop up the last bit of soup or gravy. For a traditional crusty roll, bake these on the higher temp mentioned. The lower slower bake yields a softer finish.

Ingredients

6 cups all-purpose or bread flour

2 cups warm water (110° F)

1 packet active dried yeast

1 tablespoon sugar

2 teaspoons salt

1 egg

1 tablespoon water

sesame and/or poppy seeds
  (optional)

Prep time: 3 hours, 10 minutes
Cook time: 18 minutes
Servings: 20 rolls

Instructions

1. Combine 3 cups flour, the water, yeast, and sugar in a bowl, let rest for 15 minutes. Add the remaining 3 cups of flour and salt. Knead until it forms a smooth dough (adding as little additional flour as possible). Cover and let rise for 1 hour. Knead briefly again, and let rise for another hour.

2. Preheat oven to 425° F (350° F for softer rolls).

3. Divide into 20 pieces, cover and let rise for 15 minutes. Roll each piece of dough and shape into ovals. Space the rolls evenly on a parchment-lined baking sheet, cover and let rise for 30 minutes.

4. Beat egg and water, carefully brush over the rolls. Sprinkle with sesame or poppy seeds if desired. Cut a line in the top of each roll with a sharp knife. Bake for 18 minutes (or 25 minutes at the lower temperature) or until the internal temperature is 190°F.

Sourdough rye
Chleb żytni razowy na zakwasie

Small packages of this bread were in our shopping basket every week at our Polish supermarket, until they were out of stock, week after week! And so I had to learn to make my own sourdough rye.

This is best sliced very thin. An electric slicer is perfect for the job. Instead of toasting, we like to butter both sides and fry the bread in a pan until golden brown. Whether you're having it with jam or a fried egg, it's dark and delicious!

Plan ahead! Start your flour and water mixture fermenting 5 - 6 days before you want to bake.

Ingredients

12 cups rye flour, divided
4 1/4 warm water, divided
2 1/2 teaspoons salt
1 cup hulled sunflower seeds

Prep time: 5 days (inactive), 2 1/2 hours (day of baking)
Cook time: 55 minutes
Servings: 2 loaves

Instructions

1. Mix 1/2 cup of flour and 1/4 cup of warm water in a glass vessel. Cover with a cloth and leave in a warm place for 24 hours. Repeat this process for the next 3 days, stirring in 1/2 cup of flour and 1/4 cups of water each day. Your sourdough starter will be growing for 4 days.

2. On the fifth day, transfer your starter to a large bowl and add 4 cups of rye flour and 2 1/2 cups warm water (110° F), mix and cover with a cloth and leave in a warm place for 8 hours or overnight.

3. To the dough, add 3/4 cup water and the salt. Next, add 4 cups rye flour and the sunflower seeds. Knead the dough lightly; it should still be a little sticky. Divide dough into two parchment-lined loaf pans (8- or 9-inch pans). Lightly score the top of the bread diagonally, in both directions giving a criss-cross pattern. With a pastry brush, brush the tops of the loaves with boiling water. Cover with a cloth and leave to rise in a warm place for 2 hours.

4. Preheat the oven to maximum temperature for 15 minutes, then reduce the temperature to 400° F. Brush loaves again with boiling water. Put the loaves in the oven and bake for 55 minutes. Cool before slicing. This bread stays fresh for about a week.

Rye-onion bread
Chleb żytni z cebulą

After many attempts, I've perfected a dark onion bread. This reminds me of bread always served at a favorite place in Poznań. It's ideal served with compound butter, or better yet, with a choice of compound butter.

To make your own compound butter, try stirring paprika and minced garlic (roasted garlic will have a milder taste) into softened salted butter, or you might prefer using a mixture of your favorite herbs, parsley, thyme, dill, and so on.

Ingredients

6 cups rye flour

1 packet of active dry yeast

2 teaspoons sugar

1 teaspoon salt

1 1/2 cups warm water (110° F)

1/4 cup oil or melted butter

1/4 cup dried minced onion

1 egg

1 tablespoon water

sesame and poppy seeds

Prep time: 90 minutes
Cook time: 50 minutes
Servings: 1 loaf

Instructions

1. Combine flour, yeast, sugar, salt, water, oil, and minced dried onion, stirring until uniformly combined. Cover and let rise for 1 hour.

2. Preheat the oven to 450°F. Form the dough into a loaf shape and place in a cast iron pan or on a baking stone. Beat the egg and 1 tablespoon water. Brush the loaf with the egg wash and sprinkle with seeds.

3. Bake for 10 minutes. Lower the temperature to 350° F and bake 40 more minutes or until internal temperature is 190° F.

Roll with blueberries
Jagodzianki

Who doesn't love a surprise? There is something special about filled-breads and these are no exception. Jagodzianki are vanilla and lemon-infused buns, filled with blueberries and topped with a lemon glaze! Pycha!

Prep time: 2 hours
Cook time: 15 minutes
Servings: 16 rolls

Ingredients

2 cups blueberries

1 packet of active dry yeast plus
   1 teaspoon

2/3 cup milk, divided

1/2 cup sugar, divided

1/2 cup butter

4 cup flour

1/2 teaspoon salt

1 tablespoon of vanilla extract

grated zest of 1/2 lemon

3 egg yolks

3 rounded tablespoons powdered
   sugar for the filling

1 1/2 cups powdered sugar for
   the glaze

equal amounts of water and
   lemon juice, about
   1 1/2 tablespoons each

Instructions

1. Rinse the berries and dry on a paper towel. Heat the milk to 110° F and put 4 tablespoons of the warm milk in a small glass or bowl. Add 1 tablespoon of sugar and the yeast, stir until dissolved. Let sit for about 10 minutes, it should get a little foamy.

2. Add the butter to the pan with the remaining milk, heating just enough to melt the butter; cool to room temperature. Combine the flour, salt, vanilla, lemon zest, egg yolks, milk butter mixture, and the yeast mixture mixing with a wooden spoon or a dough hook. The batter should be quite thick. Cover with a cloth and let rest for 15 minutes.

3. Turn out on a counter or pastry cloth and knead for literally, just a minute. Place in a greased bowl, turning so the top of the dough is oiled too, cover and let rise until doubled in size, 45 minutes to an hour.

4. Punch the dough down and divide into fourths. Divide each piece into fourths again, giving you 16 rolls. Using your hands, pat and pinch to shape each piece of dough into a circle about 4 inches in diameter.

5. Place 2 tablespoons blueberries on top of each roll and top berries with about 1 teaspoon of powdered sugar. Dip your finger or a pastry brush in water and lightly brush the outside edge of each dough circle as you fold and pinch the edges together to seal, tucking all of your folds underneath the bun. Place seam side down on a parchment-lined baking sheet, cover and let rest for 15 minutes, while you preheat the oven to 350° F.

6. Bake for about 15 minutes until nicely brown and remove from oven. Mix the powdered sugar with the water and lemon juice to make a glaze, spread over lukewarm buns.

Krakow pretzel
Obwarzanek krakowski

As a baker, I don't know whether to call this a pretzel or a bagel. It's similar to both. Polish friends will say it's neither. It's obwarzanek: crisp outside, soft inside, and it is synonymous with Kraków and super popular with locals and tourists alike.

Ingredients

3 3/4 cups bread flour

1 teaspoon salt

1 packet active dry yeast

1 1/4 cup warm water

3 quarts water

1 tablespoon baking soda

1 tablespoon honey

sesame seeds, poppy seeds,
   kosher salt (for toppings)

Prep time: 1 hour, 25 minutes
Cook time: 25 minutes
Servings: 6 servings

Instructions

1. Add flour, salt, yeast, and 1 1/4 cups water to a mixing bowl. Mix until well combined. Cover the bowl and let rise until doubled in size, 1 - 2 hours depending on the temperature of your room.

2. Preheat oven to 350° F. Divide dough into 6 portions. Roll one portion into a long rope, about 24 inches long. Bring the two ends together, holding the ends and what was the center. Twist until your dough is nicely spiraled. Secure the ends by pressing together, and shape into a circle or oval. Repeat to make a total of six circles.

3. Line a large baking sheet with parchment. Bring 3 quarts of water to a gentle simmer, add baking soda and honey. Gently place a circle of dough into the water, turning it after 15 - 20 seconds, lift it out and place on a parchment-lined baking sheet. Repeat with remaining 5 circles. (One of mine came "unglued" during the boiling process — no worries. I just tucked and pressed the dough back together as it went onto the baking sheet.) Top with sesame seeds, poppy seeds, or kosher salt.

4. Bake for about 20 minutes.

White bread
Chleb pszenny

Arguably, the least uniquely Polish bread in this section, after all, white bread is white bread. It's basic. It's universal. What makes it important to include when talking about Polish bread is that it's fresh, homemade, without preservatives, and it needs to be part of your bread baking repertoire.

Ingredients

5 – 6 cups flour

2 packets active dry yeast

2 teaspoons salt

2 cups milk

1/4 cup butter or oil

Prep time: 3 hours
Cook time: 45 minutes
Servings: 20

Instructions

1. Combine 2 cups flour, yeast, sugar, and salt in a mixing bowl. Heat the milk and butter until warm and the butter has melted. Cool to 110° F and add to the flour mixture. Beat until smooth. Stir in 3 more cups flour. Knead on a floured surface, adding flour as necessary for 8 – 10 minutes (or use a dough hook). The dough will be stiff.

2. Place in a greased bowl, turning the dough to grease the top. Cover and let rise for 1 – 1 1/2 hours, until doubled in size. Punch down the dough, divide in half. Shape each piece into a loaf by pressing or rolling into a 14 x 9-inch rectangle. Starting with the 9-inch side, roll tightly, sealing the edges, and place seam side down on a parchment-lined baking sheet. (The dough can be shaped and baked in greased loaf pans if you prefer.) Cover and let rise for about an hour until doubled in size.

3. Preheat the oven to 375° F. With a sharp knife, cut a diagonal slash in the top, every 3 or 4 inches. Bake in preheated oven for 40 – 45 minutes, or until golden brown and internal temperature is over 195° F. Cool before slicing.

Potato bread
Chleb ziemniaczany

Potato can be a surprising addition to baked goods in a good way. The finished product has a wonderful taste, is soft with a texture that gives something special to the tooth.

Ingredients

1 pound Russet potatoes

3 packets active dry yeast

8 cups flour

1 tablespoon salt

Prep time: 3 hours, 15 minutes
Cook time: 45 minutes
Servings: 30

Instructions

1. Wash the potatoes and bring to a boil in salted water with the skin on, or as they would say in Poland "in their uniforms." Simmer until tender and a fork can be inserted easily to the center. Reserve 2 cups of the cooking water, and allow the potatoes to cool. Peel the potatoes and rice or mash until smooth.

2. Mix the potatoes with the yeast, flour, salt, and 2 cups of the potato cooking water. If using a stand mixer and a dough hook, mix until a soft dough forms — 5-10 minutes. If using a hand mixer or wooden spoon, mix until it becomes too stiff and knead until smooth, using as little additional flour as possible.

3. Put into a large, oiled bowl and turn to grease the top of the dough. Cover and let rise for about an hour, until doubled in size. Preheat oven to 400° F. Grease 3 loaf pans. Divide dough into 3 sections and add 1 to each pan. The dough is a little soft for rolling into a loaf, but make sure it's distributed evenly across the pan and the top is relatively smooth. Cover and let rise until doubled in size, 45 minutes to 1 hour.

4. Bake for about 40 minutes, until the crust is brown and the internal temperature has reached 190° F. Cool in the pan for 10 minutes, then move to a cooling rack.

Braided egg bread
Chałka

This is a soft, enriched bread with a lightly sweet crumb topping. It's visually appealing and tastes fantastic. If you have some leftover, use it for French toast or bread pudding.

Ingredients

1 package active dry yeast

3/8 cup milk

2 tablespoon butter

6 tablespoons sugar

1 teaspoons salt

2 1/4 cups flour

1 egg

1 egg yolk

1 tablespoon water

1 tablespoon butter

1 1/2 tablespoons of sugar

1/4 cup of flour

Prep time: 2 hours
Cook time: 45 minutes
Servings: 1 loaf

Instructions

1. Sprinkle the yeast over 1/4 cup warm water (110° F) to soften, stir until dissolved. Heat milk, butter, sugar, and salt until sugar dissolves, cool to lukewarm and stir in 1 cup of flour. Add yeast and 1 egg, combine, and add enough flour to make a soft dough (another cup to 1 1/4 cups).

2. Knead on a floured surface, continuing to add flour for about 5 minutes, until the dough is smooth. Form into a ball, and place in an oiled bowl, turn the dough over (this oils the top). Cover the bowl, leave in a warm place until doubled in size about 90 minutes.

3. Punch down the dough, divide into thirds. Roll each third into an 18-inch strand and braid the three strands, securing the ends by tucking under. Place on a parchment-lined cookie sheet, cover and let rise, about 30 minutes.

4. Preheat oven to 375° F. Whisk together the egg yolk and water. In a small bowl, combine 4 teaspoons butter, 3 tablespoons of sugar, and 1/2 cup of flour to form crumb topping. Gently brush the loaf with the egg wash and sprinkle the crumb topping. The bread should be golden brown and sound hollow when tapped. Bake for 35 - 45 minutes and the internal temperature is over 195.

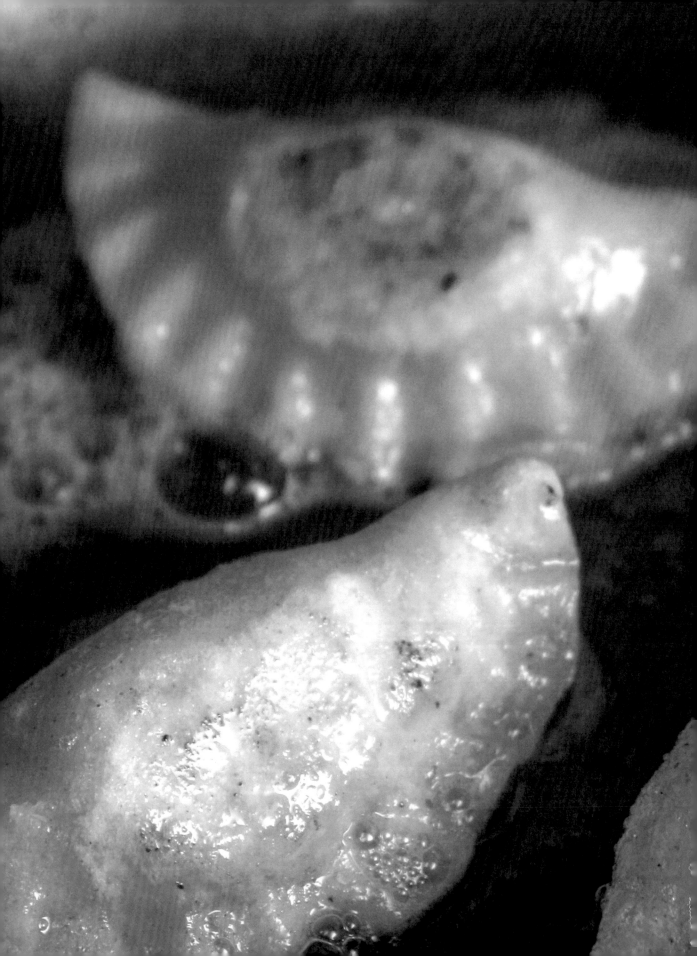

Filled dumplings | Pierogi

These lovely filled dumplings are some of the most famous items when it comes to Polish cuisine, and I would say Pierogi Ruskie (filled with a potato and cheese mixture) are at the top of the popularity list, but there are so many more varieties! There are enough filling options that some restaurants, may be called pierogarnia, devote their entire menu to pierogi.

In addition to the usual meat and savory vegetable fillings, summer brings an abundance of fresh fruit and fruit-filled pierogi.

Most often pierogi are boiled and sometimes sautéed afterwards, but there are also baked pierogi. The baked version uses a yeast dough for the crust and they tend to be larger than their pasta pierogi cousins.

Traditional pierogi dough | Tradycyjne ciasto na pierogi

Baked pierogi dough (a yeast dough) | Pieczone pierogi
(ciasto drożdżowe)

Pork pierogi | Pierogi z mięsem wieprzowym

Potato and cheese pierogi | Pierogi ruskie

Spinach pierogi | Pierogi ze szpinakiem

Cabbage and mushroom pierogi | Pierogi z kapustą i grzybów

Mixed berry pierogi | Pierogi z jagodami

Strawberry pierogi| Pierogi z truskawkami

Ingredients

1 2/3 cups flour

9 tablespoons water

1 tablespoon butter

2 pinches salt

Prep time: 40 minutes
Cook time: 20 minutes
Servings: 2 dozen pierogi

Instructions

1. Place the flour in a mixing bowl. Heat the water until it just begins to boil, and add the butter to the hot water. As soon as the butter has melted, add the water and butter mixture and the salt to the flour. Stir with a wooden spoon until everything is combined, cover, and let rest about 15 minutes.

2. You can prepare the filling (of your choice) while the dough rests.

3. Knead the dough for a few minutes, until smooth, but only use a pinch of flour – minimal flour should be added. Roll out 1/4 of the dough to about 1/8 inch thick, picking it up and turning the dough occasionally, but be careful to always put the same side down. Don't flip the dough. Sprinkle a pinch of flour to the top if necessary to keep the rolling pin from sticking.

4. Cut dough into circles using a large water glass 3 to 3.5 inches in diameter. Use the underside of the circles for the center of your pierogi, placing about a teaspoon of filling (of your choice) in the center. Pinch the center of the edges together, and crimp the remainder in the pattern of your choice (there are inspiring YouTube videos). Cook in boiling (salted) water according to your filling instructions. For an uncooked meat filling, cook for five minutes (check a sample pieróg to be sure it's cooked by cutting into it), for vegetable, fruit, or precooked meat fillings, cook just until they rise to the top of the boiling water.

5. After boiling, you may sauté your pierogi in melted butter. Serve with sour cream, sauteed onions, and/or bacon (on the side if you like).

Traditional pierogi dough
Tradycyjne ciasto na pierogi

This is one of many wonderful pierogi dough recipes. It's eggless. The secret to getting a good seal on your pierogi is to not work in too much flour. In the process of rolling out your dough, always leave the same side down; it's OK if the bottom is just a little bit sticky. Sprinkle minimal flour during the rolling process. When you cut circles in your dough, make the bottom the inside of your pieróg.

The recipe makes about two dozen because you can make a small batch for a meal. You don't have to always make enormous quantities every time you make pierogi. If you do need to make a huge batch, just multiply to get the desired quantity.

Baked pierogi dough (a yeast dough)
Pieczone pierogi (ciasto drożdżowe)

Baked pierogi are less common, but this recipe could change that! It is delicious. I love that these larger pierogi provide more room for fillings or even a combination of fillings. Of the many combinations I tried, I think pork and sauerkraut with mushroom are the winning combination!

Ingredients

3 1/2 cups flour
1 packet dry yeast
1 teaspoon sugar
pinch of salt
3 tablespoons butter
1 cup milk
2 eggs, divided

Prep time: 15 minutes
Cook time: 20 minutes
Servings: 12-18 large pierogi

Instructions

1. Combine the flour, yeast, sugar, salt, and butter, cutting in the butter. Then add 1 egg and the milk. Mix the dough, kneading if it seems too stiff. Add a little more flour if it's too sticky. The dough should be soft, not too hard or sticky.

2. Roll out quite thin, about 1/8 inch thick. Cut into circles 4 - 6 inches in diameter. Add your desired filling, making your pierogi as full as possible with 3 - 6 teaspoons of filling. Seal the edges, brushing with a little water if necessary, pinching and fluting or sealing with a fork. Place on a parchment-lined baking sheet, seam up or seam to the side. Let the dumplings rest for 15 minutes

3. While the dumplings rest, preheat oven to 350° F. Beat the remaining egg with 2 tablespoons of water. Brush the egg wash over the dumplings. Bake for 20 minutes, until brown.

Pork pierogi
Pierogi z mięsem wieprzowym

A hearty meat filling with subtly interesting spices.

Ingredients

6 ounces ground pork

1/2 teaspoon salt

1 teaspoon Pieprz Ziołowy*

¼ cup finely diced onion

2 teaspoons oil or lard

***Pieprz Ziołowy** adds a variety of flavors and depth to recipes, also try it in soups. You'll find it on Amazon, maybe in Polish delis, or you can make your own:

2 tablespoons sweet paprika

1 tablespoon coriander seeds

1 tablespoon white mustard seeds

2 teaspoons cumin seeds

1 1/2 teaspoons dried marjoram

6 small bay leaves

1/4 teaspoon cayenne

1/3 teaspoon garlic powder

Grind to a powder with mortar and pestle or in a spice grinder. .

Prep time: 30 minutes
Cook time: 20 minutes
Servings: 2 dozen

Instructions

1. Add the pork, salt, and Pieprz Ziołowy to a mixing bowl. Sauté the onion in oil until translucent. Add to the pork and mix until the onions and seasonings are evenly distributed.

2. Fill 3 inch circles of your favorite pierogi dough with a teaspoon of the pork filling. Cook in simmering water for 5 minutes. You might finish by sautéing in butter or serve with melted butter. Other options include serving with sour cream or sauteed diced onion.

Potato and cheese pierogi
Pierogi ruskie

This filling is an international favorite. Also called pierogi ruskie, many assume this means Russian pierogi, but it actually means Rusyn pierogi. Rusyns (also know as Carpat ho-Rusyns) are an ethnic group who now live mostly in Ukraine and Slovakia.

Ingredients

1 1/2 pounds of potatoes

2 tablespoons butter

3/4 cup diced onion

1 1/4 cups twaróg* (can substitute ricotta or cottage cheese)

salt and pepper, to taste

smoked bacon, diced, for garnish

recipe for twaróg can be found at polishhousewife.com/twarog-polish-farmers-cheese/

Prep time: 20 minutes
Cook time: 40 minutes
Servings: 2-3 dozen

Instructions

1. Boil the potatoes until tender, then peel and rice. Place riced potatoes into a large bowl. Sautee onions in butter until light brown. Lightly toss potatoes, with onion, cheese, and seasonings until combined.

2. Wrap circles of your favorite pierogi dough around a teaspoon of the filling, seal the edges and cook in simmering salted water until the pierogi rise to the top of the water.

3. After boiling the pierogi, you might serve with melted butter, sautéed bacon and onion, or sour cream. If you prefer, sauté the pierogi after boiling, and add any combination of toppings.

Spinach pierogi
Pierogi ze szpinakiem

This creamed spinach filling is so delicious that you won't mind if you have more filling than needed. Other than the cream cheese, use whatever cheeses you have on hand. Enjoy it as a side dish or a warm dip.

Ingredients

1 tablespoon butter

1 shallot, minced

2 cloves garlic, minced

16 ounces frozen spinach, cooked and drained

6 ounces cream cheese

1/2 cup grated Parmesan cheese

1 ounce Havarti cheese

salt, pepper, nutmeg (to taste)

Prep time: 40 minutes
Cook time: 20 minutes
Servings: 4 dozen

Instructions

1. Add butter, shallot, and garlic to a pan and sauté until translucent. Add cooked and drained spinach, cream cheese, Parmesan cheese, and Havarti. Season with salt, pepper, and nutmeg.

2. Heat until cheeses are melted and well combined. Other than the cream cheese, use any combination of cheeses; the Parmesan and Havarti were just what we had on hand and enjoy

3. Season to taste with salt, pepper, and nutmeg and allow the filling to cool before filling pierogi.

4. Cook pierogi in simmering salted water until they float to the top. Sauté in butter (optional).

Cabbage and mushroom pierogi
Pierogi z kapustą i grzybów

This sort of meatless pierogi usually makes an appearance on Christmas Eve, but don't limit it to just one night a year. The flavors are amazing, and this filling deserves to be a year-round star!

Ingredients

4 cups mushrooms

1 carrot

3 tablespoons fresh parsley, minced

2 tablespoons butter

1 pound sauerkraut

salt and pepper

Prep time: 40 minutes
Cook time: 20 minutes
Servings: 2 dozen pierogi

Instructions

1. Dice mushrooms, shred carrot and sauté with the parsley in butter until mushrooms are golden.

2. Drain sauerkraut, add to a saucepan and cover with water and simmer for 20 minutes, drain the sauerkraut.

3. Run mushroom mixture and sauerkraut through a meatgrinder or finely process in a food processor. Season with salt and pepper. Use to fill your favorite pierogi dough. Cook in simmering water salted water until pierogi float to the top.

Mixed berry pierogi
Pierogi z jagodami

This mixed berry concoction has a beautiful color and the brightest fruity taste. They're a twist on pierogi z borowkami (blueberry pierogi). The combination of berries and the pierogi dough reminds me of boysenberry syrup and pancakes.

Ingredients

3 cups mixed berries, for example blueberries, raspberries, and blackberries

3/4 cup water

1/3 cup sugar

1/2 teaspoon cinnamon

1 teaspoon lemon juice

5 - 6 tablespoons bread crumbs

Prep time: 40 minutes
Cook time: 20 minutes
Servings: 40 pierogi

Instructions

1. Combine berries, water, sugar, cinnamon, and lemon juice; bring to a boil and simmer approximately 20 minutes. The berries will break down. Add bread crumbs and continue to simmer until thickened.

2. Refrigerate until chilled and more firm; it's easier to wrap the dough around a firm filling. Assemble as usual. You can eat these after boiling or saute in butter after boiling. We like to finish them with a dipping sauce of sour cream and brown sugar.

Strawberry pierogi
Pierogi z truskawkami

While some tell me they have never heard of sweet pierogi, it's just one of the many ways Poles enjoy fresh fruit in the summer. Polish strawberries are loved by all who try them. To me, they seem a little more like wild strawberries than the large cultivated berries I see in the United States. They are smaller and juicier. The perfect filling for pierogi!

Ingredients

24 small strawberries, probably a
   heaping cup
powdered sugar to garnish

Prep time: 5 minutes
Cook time: 15 minutes
Servings: 2 dozen pierogi

Instructions

1. Prepare pierogi dough, top with strawberry, Fold your favorite pierogi dough over the berry and crimp.

2. Carefully place in simmering salted water, cook until they float to the top. Saute in butter if you like. Serve with sour cream and brown sugar or whipped cream.

Main dishes | Dania główne

The first and last meal of the day are often very light, and sometimes identical: cold cuts, a slice of cheese, and bread. So most of the recipes listed here are hearty dishes that would be eaten for dinner or obiad, the large afternoon meal. These are the wonderful smells that waft up the stairwell in an apartment building every afternoon!

Goulash| Gulasz

Hunter's stew | Bigos

Cabbage rolls | Gołąbki

Pork cutlet | Kotlet schabowy

Pork rolls | Bułki wieprzowe

Smoked Polish sausage | Kiełbasa wędzona

Goulash
Gulasz

A big scoop of gulasz on top of potato pancakes is one of my favorite meals, but potato pancakes aren't your only option to accompany this pepper and paprika stew. Try it over noodles, rice, or the very Polish buckwheat kasza. Gulasz is **so** full of flavor. The leftovers are great too. A potato pancake, gulasz, and a fried egg for breakfast is a delicious start to the day.

Ingredients

2 pounds pork, trimmed and diced

3/4 cup flour

kosher salt

black pepper

3 tablespoons olive oil

1 cup chopped onion

2 bell peppers, cut into thin strips

2 cloves garlic, minced

14 ounces broth, pork, beef,
   or veggie

2 tablespoons tomato paste

4 tablespoons paprika

1/4 teaspoon black pepper

6 whole allspice

1/4 cup dry red wine

1/3 cup cold water

3 tablespoons flour

potato pancakes, cooked
   according to directions

Prep time: 20 minutes
Cook time: 2 hours
Servings: 6 servings

Instructions

1. Dredge pork in 3/4 cup flour that has been generously seasoned with salt and pepper. In a large saucepan, brown pork cubes in hot oil; do 2 or 3 separate batches. Set browned pork aside and brown onions and peppers, add garlic at the end. (After multiple batches of meat and then the veggies, there will likely be a dark brown crust on the bottom of the pan. Don't worry, it will loosen and dissolve in the liquids you're about to add – giving you a dark, flavorful broth.)

2. Return pork to the pan and add broth, tomato paste, paprika, pepper, allspice and wine. Simmer covered 60 to 90 minutes.

3. In a small bowl, blend water and 3 tablespoons flour. Add to meat mixture to thicken. Simmer 15 to 30 minutes, stirring occasionally.

4. Serve over potato pancakes, noodles, rice, or buckwheat kasza.

Hunter's stew
Bigos

Traditionally, this would have been made with bear and wild boar, so if you have some hunter friends, this is the time to pull the game meat they've given you out of the freezer. Bigos is sure to be served at every festival, and people in the know say it has to be reheated a time or two to be at its best.

Ingredients

1/2 pound pork, diced
1/2 pound beef, diced
salt and pepper
3 tablespoons olive oil
4 medium onions, sliced
1 pound slab bacon, diced
2 cups beef broth
8 ounce container
   mushrooms, sliced
2 pounds sauerkraut, drained
   and rinsed
4 apples, peeled, cored and grated
1/2 cup pitted prunes, quartered
32 ounces canned diced tomatoes
1 tablespoon caraway seeds
12 peppercorns
1 pound Polish sausage, quartered
   lengthwise and sliced
2 bay leaves
1/2 pound ham, diced
1/2 cup dry red wine

Prep time: 30 minutes
Cook time: 2 1/2 hours
Servings: 6-8 servings

Instructions

1. Season the pork and beef with salt and pepper. Add olive oil to a large Dutch oven and saute the meat and onions in batches, cooking until the meat is browned and the onions begin to caramelize. Brown the bacon.

2. Combine all the ingredients, and simmer at least two hours, or overnight.

3. Serve as is, over noodles, with buckwheat kasza or with crusty bread.

Cabbage rolls
Gołąbki

Cabbage rolls are the only Polish dish I had in my recipe line up before we moved to Poland. There are many variations. Some use a tomato soup for their sauce, some use a brown gravy, or even bake them without sauce. Serve them with mashed potatoes and you have a hearty, comforting meal.

Ingredients

2/3 cup white rice

2 heads green cabbage

2 eggs, beaten

1 1/2 pounds ground beef

1 cup chopped onion

1 teaspoon salt

1/4 teaspoon pepper

8 slices bacon, cut in 1-inch pieces

2 16-ounce cans tomatoes

2 8-ounce cans tomato sauce

2 bay leaves

Prep time: 30 minutes
Cook time: 2 1/2 hours
Servings: 8 servings

Instructions

1. Cook rice according to package directions, cool. Remove the core from cabbage; run hot water into cored area to help in removing outer leaves (or if you plan ahead, freeze the cabbage, the leaves will come off easily and be ready to roll after you thaw the cabbage). Remove 8 - 12 leaves from each head of cabbage; chop remaining cabbage and place in two baking dishes (or a large Dutch oven). Sprinkle the chopped cabbage with salt.

2. Boil cabbage leaves until limp, about 5 minutes, drain and rinse in cold water. Cut about 2 inches of the heavy center vein from the leaves.

3. Cook bacon with 1/2 cup onion till bacon is crisp. Stir in undrained tomatoes, tomato sauce, and bay leaf. Simmer, covered, while preparing the rest of the dish. Remove bay leaves before adding to the dish.

3. Combine cooked rice, egg, ground beef, the remaining 1/2 cup onion, salt, and pepper; mix well. Place about 1/4 cup rice mixture in center of each cabbage leaf; fold in sides and roll ends over rice. Place the cabbage rolls seam side down, on top of chopped cabbage. Pour tomato mixture over cabbage rolls. Cover and bake at 350 degrees from 1 1/4 to 1 1/2 hours. Freezes well.

Pork cutlet
Kotlet schabowy

Thin cutlets cook quickly ensuring the pork stays moist with a crisp coating. They're heavenly!

Ingredients

4 boneless pork chops

salt and pepper

3/4 cup flour

2 eggs, beaten

1 cup bread crumbs

1/3 cup oil, more if needed

Prep time: 20 minutes
Cook time: 10 minutes
Servings: 4 servings

Instructions

1. Preheat oven to 350° F. Place pork chops on a cutting board and pound them flat, about 1/4 inch thick (they'll be twice as big after the pounding). Season the flattened chops with salt and pepper.

2. Set up three plates. Put flour in the first, beaten eggs in the second, and breadcrumbs in the third. Dredge the first cutlet with flour, then dip both sides in egg, then bread crumbs. Set aside and repeat with the three remaining cutlets.

3. Heat the oil in a frying pan over medium-high heat to 350° F. Add cutlets to the pan without crowding, it may take more than one batch. Cook on both sides, just until golden brown. Place on a paper towel-lined baking sheet and pop in the oven for about 5 minutes. This ensures the meat is cooked and they're all hot when served.

Pork rolls
Bułki wieprzowe or Rolady z karkówki

You can also make these meat rolls with beef or poultry. Cooked and served in gravy, just add your favorite potato dish.

Ingredients

8 small pork cutlets

2 teaspoon salt, divided

1 teaspoon pepper, divided

2 tablespoons mustard

8 thin slices ham, or strips of bacon

4 small dill gherkins, quartered lengthwise

3 tablespoons finely diced onion

4 tablespoons oil

2 tablespoons flour

1 cup broth

1/4 cup wine (red or white)

1 tablespoon tomato paste

toothpicks or skewers

Prep time: 20 minutes
Cook time: 1 hour, 10 minutes
Servings: 4 servings

Instructions

1. Using a meat tenderizer, flatten the pork cutlets until they are 1/4 inch thick. Sprinkle with 1 teaspoon salt and 1/2 teaspoon pepper. Turn the cutlets over and spread with mustard. Top with a slice of ham or bacon, two small pickle spears, and a sprinkle of diced onion.

2. Roll up the pork, wrapping all of the toppings inside. Secure with a toothpick. Heat the oil in a Dutch oven or large frying pan. Brown the pork rolls on all sides.

3. Remove pork from the pan. Add the flour to the pan and cook until it begins to brown. Slowly whisk in broth. Add wine and tomato paste. Return pork to the pan and simmer covered for an hour, adding more broth if needed. Serve with gravy.

Smoked Polish sausage
Kiełbasa wędzona

This is without a doubt the most delicious sausage! Use it in your favorite recipes, or nibble it straight, hot or cold. This requires more special equipment than most recipes. You'll need a meat grinder, a sausage stuffer (this can be a mixer attachment or a separate device), and a smoker.

Ingredients

Hog casings, 32-35 mm

4 pounds pork shoulder roast

1 pound pork fat or bacon

5-10 cloves garlic, minced

2 tablespoons kosher or sea salt

2 teaspoons dried marjoram

2 teaspoons sugar

2 teaspoons black pepper

1 teaspoon Instacure #1 pink salt

1 cup of ice-cold water

Prep time: 1 day (3 hours active)
Cook time: 4-5 hours
Servings: 20 servings (5 pounds)

Instructions

1. Soak the hog casings in water for 1-2 hours, changing the water a few times. When the casings are pliable, run water through the casings. You want to remove all of the salt.

2. While the casings are soaking, dice the pork into 1 1/2 inch chunks. They need to be small enough to fit in your meat grinder. Do the same with the pork fat or bacon. Put the pork in a single layer on a baking sheet (you might need more than one) and sprinkle the pork fat or bacon over the diced pork. Put the trays into the freezer for about 2 hours. The meat needs to be very firm, beginning to get stiff. It makes it so much easier to grind.

3. Combine the garlic, salt, marjoram, sugar, pepper, and pink salt; set aside. Grind the meat using a grinding plate with 1/4 or 5/16 inch holes, or the closest you have. Add the ground meat to a mixing bowl, sprinkle with the seasonings, and mix with very clean hands, a wooden spoon, or the paddle attachment of a stand mixer. Mix in the cold water.

4. Load the casings onto the stuffing horn (tube) of your sausage stuffer. Leave a couple of inches loose. Begin to process the meat, stopping the stuffer just as the sausage starts to move from the tube to the casing. Tie a knot in the loose casing as close as possible to the sausage. Process slowly. Stop the sausage stuffer, every 15-18 inches, stop the stuffer, slide an inch of casing off the tube, rotate the sausage a few times to twist the slack casing. Tie a short length of twine around the twisted casing.

5. Place the sausage, uncovered, in the refrigerator to air dry overnight. Remove the sausage from the fridge for an hour or two to bring it to room temperature. Hang the sausage over dowels and add to your smoker. At this point the dampers should be wide open and the temp at 120° to 130° F without smoke for 30 minutes. This is to ensure your sausage casings are dry.

6. Move the dampers to 1/4 open and slowly increase the heat to no more than 165° and add smoke. Monitor the temperature closely because you don't want to melt the fat in your sausage if it gets too high. Your sausage needs to come to an internal temperature of 152°. This can take as long as 10 hours. As the internal temperature rises, it takes longer and longer to increase by another degree. You can smoke your sausage to an internal temperature of 140° and then move it to your stovetop in a steamer. Steam for only 2-3 minutes, keeping a close eye on the internal temperature. Your goal is still only 152°, and we don't want the fat to melt. Spray with cold water to stop the cooking process. Air dry in the fridge overnight.

Note: there will be a little sausage left in your stuffer when you're finished. Shape this into a patty and fry this up now to sample, but know that the flavors will be even better when the process is finished. Your smoked sausage will keep in the fridge for a week or in a vacuum-sealed bag in the freezer for up to a year.

Side dishes | Przystawki

Side dishes, some of which you might also see as appetizers, are often the favorite part of a meal. That holds true with this selection. I could make a meal of any of these! For the most part, these recipes are based on the vegetables that grow well in Poland's long summer days and have an extended shelf life to keep people going until the next harvest.

Potato pancakes | Placki ziemniaczane

Cabbage salad | Sałatka z bialej kapusty

Red cabbage | Czerwona kapusta

Cucumbers in sour cream | Mizeria

Potato salad | Sałatka jarzynowa

Sour pickles | Ogórki kiszone

Sauerkraut | Kapusta kiszona

Lard spread | Smalec

Potato dumplings | Kopytka

Beet salad | Sałatka z buraków

Potato pancakes
Placki ziemniaczane

Potato pancakes are comfort food: they taste like love. I like to top them with gulasz, but I've heard of people eating them with everything from grape jelly to sour cream.

Ingredients

1 1/2 pounds of potatoes

1 small onion

1 small egg

2 tablespoons flour

1 teaspoon salt

1/4 teaspoon pepper

oil for frying

Prep time: 15 minutes
Cook time: 15 minutes
Servings: 9 pancakes

Instructions

1. Peel potatoes and grate on the fine side of the grater, or you can process in a blender or food processor. Shredded potatoes (the large holes on the box grater) work also, it's really a matter of individual preference. Grate onion. Put the potatoes and onion in a colander, press with paper towels to drain.

2. In a bowl, beat egg; stir in flour, salt, and pepper until smooth. Add drained potatoes and onion, stirring until well combined. Heat oil 1/4-inch, in frying pan over medium-high heat. Melted lard would be a traditional choice, but peanut oil is another excellent choice for frying.

3. Add 1/4 cup of the potato mixture to the hot oil. Use the back of a spoon to spread the batter until the pancake is about 1/2 inch thick. The size of your frying pan will determine how many you can cook at one time.

4. Cook 2 to 3 minutes on each side. My frying pan is larger than the largest burner, so I also rotate them halfway through each side so the whole pancake is evenly cooked. Drain on paper towels.

Cabbage salad
Sałatka z białej kapusty

Lighter than coleslaw, this Polish classic is the perfect side dish for any meal. It adds a bit of crunch and a hint of dill. I love the way it combines sweet and savory ingredients.

Ingredients

1 small head cabbage, finely shredded

juice of one lemon

1 teaspoon salt

1 apple, shredded

1/2 teaspoon dill seed

dash of garlic powder

1 tablespoon powdered sugar (granulated will work too)

1/2 cup vegetable oil

1 small carrot, grated (optional)

Prep time: 15 minutes
Cook time: 4 hours
Servings: 12 servings

Instructions

1. Mix the cabbage with the lemon juice and salt. Let stand for 4 hours or refrigerate overnight. The acid and salt will begin to chemically cook the cabbage, softening it a bit.

2. Add the apple, dill seed, garlic powder, sugar, oil, and carrot (optional). Toss lightly.

Red cabbage
Czerwona kapusta

This sweet and sour red cabbage adds a wonderful pop of color to any plate. The finished product freezes well, so make the full recipe and enjoy it twice.

Ingredients

1 onion, diced

2 tart apples, peeled, cored and diced

3 tablespoons butter

1 head red cabbage

1/2 cup vinegar

1/3 cup sugar

1 1/2 teaspoons salt

1/2 teaspoon pepper

1/2 cup seedless blackberry preserves

Prep time: 15 minutes
Cook time: 1 hour, 20 minutes
Servings: 12 servings

Instructions

1. In a large Dutch oven, saute onion and apples in butter until soft.

2. Cut cabbage into quarters, remove the core and outer leaves, thinly slice remaining leaves to produce a finely shredded cabbage.

3. Add cabbage, vinegar, sugar, salt, and pepper to pan, cook approximately one hour, until cabbage is soft, stirring occasionally. Stir in blackberry preserves, combine over heat until the preserves are melted.

Cucumbers in sour cream
Mizeria

A refreshing salad of cucumbers and sour cream – it's a summer staple.

Ingredients

2 cucumbers

salt

1/2 cup sour cream

2 tablespoons vinegar

1 tablespoon finely cut chives
  or green onions

1 tablespoon finely cut fresh dill

1 teaspoon sugar

1/2 teaspoon salt

1/4 teaspoon black pepper

Prep time: 10 minutes
Cook time: 20 minutes
Servings: 4 servings

Instructions

1. For ordinary cucumbers, peel, slice lengthwise and remove the seeds. Slice as thin as possible, no more than 1/8 inch. If you're using the thin-skinned hothouse cucumbers or pickling cukes, just slice.

2. Spread out the slices and sprinkle with salt. After 20 minutes pat and press with a paper towel.

3. Combine the sour cream, vinegar, chives, dill, sugar, 1/2 teaspoon salt, and pepper. Chill.

Potato salad
Sałatka jarzynowa

Whether you call it potato salad, vegetable salad, or root vegetable salad, this recipe is a real crowd pleaser. It is one of the most popular recipes on my web site.

Ingredients

1 large or 2 leeks, white part only, carefully rinsed

1/2 cup finely chopped flat-leaf parsley

2 1/2 teaspoons salt, divided

1 tablespoon olive oil

8 medium potatoes

6 carrots

1 small to medium celery root (or 1/2 large)

1 dozen eggs, hard-boiled

4 cups shredded dill pickles (large side of grater), press out the juice

1 1/2 cup mayonnaise

1/2 teaspoon black pepper

Prep time: 1 hour, 40 minutes
Cook time: 40 minutes
Servings: 12-14 servings

Instructions

1. Finely dice the leek and combine with parsley, 1 teaspoon salt and olive oil: set aside (this softens the leek).

2. Add whole potatoes, carrots, and celery root to a large Dutch oven. Cover with salted water, bring to a boil, reduce heat to simmer, and cook until tender (a fork can be inserted easily) 30-40 minutes. Drain, cool.

3. Peel the cooked vegetables, diced into 1/3 inch (1 cm) cubes. Dice egg whites, and crumble the yolks. Add all of this to a large bowl; add pickles, mayo, remaining 1 1/2 teaspoon salt, and black pepper.

4. Cover and keep refrigerated. You can "frost" with additional mayo if desired.

Sour pickles
Ogórki kiszone

My Polish friends would correct the name I've given this recipe – I've been told more than once that pickles are made with vinegar. These are preserved cucumbers, and they are much beloved in Poland.

Ingredients

wide mouth 1-quart jar

8 - 10 pickling cucumbers (4-6 inches long), washed and dried

2 tablespoons pickling salt or sea salt

1-quart water

2 teaspoons mustard seeds

2 cloves peeled garlic

1 stem dill, preferably flowering

fresh horseradish root, about 1 inch long

bay leaf

cherry, grape, blackcurrant, or oak leaf

Prep time: 20 minutes
Cook time: 1-3 weeks (inactive)
Servings: 1 quart

Instructions

1. Tightly pack the cucumbers into the sterile jar. You'll want to squeeze them in so they'll stay submerged and not float to the top of the liquid.

2. Add the salt to the water and bring to a boil.

3. Add the mustard seeds, garlic, dill (fold to fit), horseradish, bay leaf, and other leaf if you have one, to the jar with the cukes.

4. Fill the jar with the saltwater to within 1/4 inch from the top; all of your ingredients should be covered. Loosely cap the jar with a sterile lid; the lid must be loose to allow the gases produced during fermentation to escape. Some brine may seep out so store where this won't be a problem.

Note: As it ferments, the brine will become cloudy. Depending on your taste, the cucumbers will be ready to eat in 1 to 3 weeks. Fermentation will end after 5-6 weeks, if you have any left at this point, the lids should be tightened to prevent spoilage.

Prep time: 10 minutes
Cook time: 4-14 days (inactive)
Servings: 32 servings

Ingredients

5 pounds cabbage

½ pound carrots

7 1/2 teaspoons sea salt
   (no iodine)

Instructions

1. Discard the outer layers of cabbage that tend to be dirty or bruised. Rinse the cabbage and cut out the core. Carefully remove 1-2 large leaves and set aside. Cut the cabbage into quarters. Slice the cabbage very thinly. Peel and shred the carrots.

2. Place the veggies in a large bowl, layering with the salt. Toss and massage the mixture vigorously with your very clean or gloved hands (you don't want to introduce stray bacteria into the fermentation process). You can use the end of a rolling pin (one that doesn't have a handle), or the wooden pressing tool from your meat grinder in this process. You need the cabbage to release a lot of liquid. The volume should be reduced by half. Let it rest for 15 minutes.

3. Squeeze the liquid out of the vegetables, save the liquid. Add the veggies to your fermentation crock or quart jars. Pack them down and cover the top with the large leaves you set aside in step 1. Tuck the leaf in around the edges if possible. This is to keep little bits of cabbage from floating to the top. Add your weights to the crock. (I've swapped out the ceramic weights that came with my crock for glass weights.)

4. Pour the reserved brine into the crock or jar. You need 2 inches on top of the veggies. Add enough brine (1 cup water to 1 teaspoon salt) to bring it up to that level. Fill the ring with water and add the lid. It will take 2 days for things to start fermenting. After that, push everything down every day to release air pockets that will form. Your kapusta will be ready in 4 - 14 days depending on the temperature in your room. Seal in clean quart jars and refrigerate.

Sauerkraut
Kapusta kiszona

I used a 10 liter crock, but you could do this in 4 or 5 quart jars, using a freezer bag filled with water to keep the cabbage submerged. The key thing to remember is to use 1 1/2 teaspoons of salt for every pound of cabbage and keep the cabbage submerged in brine. I know Polish cooks who think nothing of chopping up 40 Kg of cabbage to ferment. Such a big commitment isn't necessary.

Lard spread
Smalec

It surprised me how much I love smalec, the flavors, the texture, the contrast of the smalec and pickle. It's a delightful experience all around. Often served as an appetizer, smalec is also something to nibble on late into the night when you find yourself sharing a drink and deep thoughts with dear friends. It goes especially well with beer or vodka.

Ingredients

2 1/2 pounds pork fat, coarsely ground or finely diced*

1/2 pounds bacon, coarsely ground or finely diced

3 medium onions (about 3 1/2 cups), finely diced

4 cloves garlic, minced

1 teaspoon salt

1/4 teaspoon black pepper

1 teaspoon marjoram

2 Granny Smith apples, peeled, cores, and grated or finely diced

*You can find large quantities of pork fat at specialty butcher shops. You can also ask the butcher at your local supermarket to save scraps of pork fat for you. This makes a lot but it freezes well. It's nice to be able to just pull a ramekin out of the freezer when you know guests are coming.

Prep time: 20 minutes
Cook time: 1 hour
Servings: 24 servings

Instructions

1. In a large frying pan, cook the ground pork fat for 10 minutes over medium heat, it will begin to render fat. Add the ground bacon, onions, garlic, salt, and pepper. Stir, scraping the bottom frequently.

2. Reduce heat to low, cooking and stirring for another 50 minutes until the rendered fat level begins to be higher than than the chopped bits in the pan. Add the marjoram and grated apple.

3. Cool to room temperature, stirring occasionally for uniform consistency. Store in the fridge.

4. Serve with dark bread and small dill pickles.

Potato dumplings
Kopytka

This is one of the most popular Polish potato dumplings. Serve them with buttered bread crumbs or gravy.

Ingredients

1 pound potatoes

1/2 teaspoon salt

1 egg

2 cups flour

Prep time: 30 minutes

Cook time: 45 minutes

Servings: 4

Instructions

1. With the skins on, boil potatoes until tender. Cool, and then peel the potatoes.

2. Bring a large pot of salted water to a simmer.

3. Mash the potatoes thoroughly or process with a potato ricer. Stir in the egg and salt. Add enough flour to create a smooth dough, stirring just enough to incorporate the flour. Overworking will make for tough dumplings.

4. Take a small amount of the dough and roll on a floured surface to form a rope about 3/4 inch in diameter. Slice the rope on the diagonal about 1/2 inch apart. Boil in salted water about 4 minutes without overcrowding the pan; you'll do multiple batches. Remove from the water with a slotted spoon.

5. Serve topped with buttered bread crumbs, pan drippings, gravy or sugar.

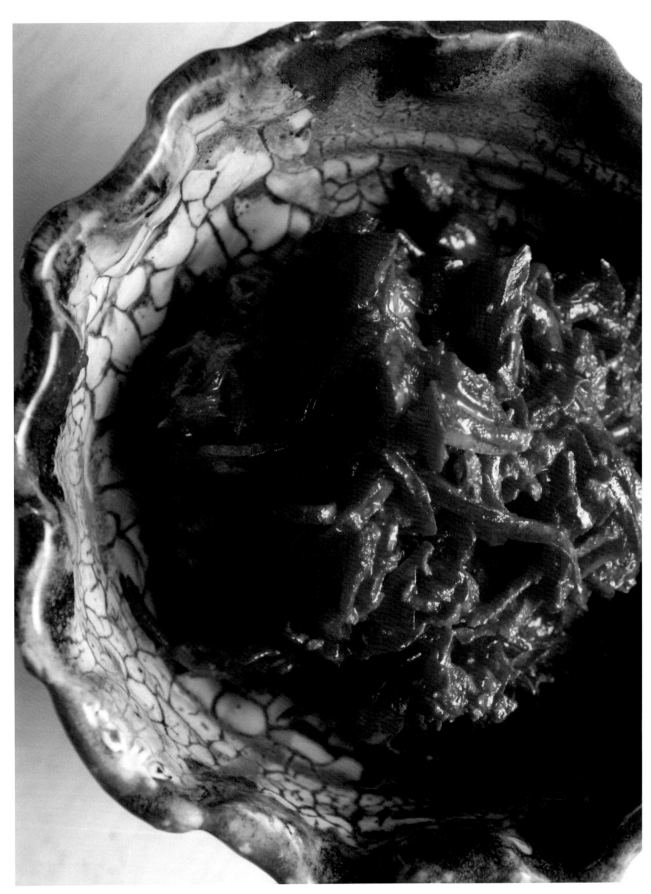

Beet salad
Sałatka z buraków

The predominant flavors in this salad, beets and horseradish, can be simple; just stir a dab of prepared horse-radish into shredded, roasted beets. But this recipe kicks it up a notch with layers of supporting flavors.

Ingredients

3 large beets
1 small onion, finely diced
1 Granny Smith apple, shredded
2 dill pickles, shredded
2 tablespoons oil
2 tablespoons mayonnaise
2 teaspoons horseradish
1 teaspoon sugar
1 teaspoon salt
1/2 teaspoon pepper

Prep time: 30 minutes
Cook time: 90 minutes
Servings: 6 servings

Instructions

1. Preheat oven to 350° F. Trim the leaves and the root tip from the beets. Wrap each beet in aluminum foil. Bake for 60-90 minutes until the beets are tender — you should be able to insert a fork easily into the middle of the beets. Unwrap and soak in cold water until they're cool enough to peel. The peel will come off easily. Shred the beets using the large hole side of a grater.

2. Combine the beets with onion, apple, pickle, oil, mayo, horseradish, sugar, salt, and pepper.

3. Serve at room temperature or chilled.

Desserts | Desery

For an American palate, Polish desserts are noticeably less sweet, letting the flavor of the other ingredients shine. For example, Szarlotka tastes more like apples than my American apple pie. There is some sugar in the crust, but my szarlotka filling is only fruit with a dash of cinnamon. Not only are the desserts less sweet, they're served in smaller portions than we're used to seeing. That way, dessert can be enjoyed regularly.

Gingerbread cookies | Pierniczki

Gingerbread cake | Ciasto imbirowe

Rhubarb crumb cake| Ciasto z rabarbarem i kruszonką

Apple pie | Szarlotka

Poppy seed roll | Makowiec

Apple fritters | Słodkie placuszki z jabłkiem

St. Martin's croissants | Rogale świętomarcińskie

Crepes with cheese filling | Naleśniki z serem

Gingerbread cookies
Pierniczki

Originating from the town of Toruń, home of Nicolaus Copernicus, pierniczki are a crisp, lightly spiced cookie prepared in a variety of ways. Leave the cookies plain or top with icing and your favorite decorations. They're done up here for Valentine's Day, saying "I love you."

Ingredients

1/4 cup honey

1/3 cup butter

1/2 cup brown sugar

1 large egg

2 1/4 cups flour (you might like to try rye flour)

1 teaspoon baking soda

1 teaspoon cinnamon

1 teaspoon ground ginger

1 teaspoon cocoa

1/4 teaspoon salt

Prep time: 30 minutes
Cook time: 24 minutes
Servings: 4 dozen small cookies

Instructions

1. Preheat oven to 350° F. In a saucepan, heat the honey, butter, and brown sugar over medium heat until the butter melts and sugar dissolves. Remove from heat, cool if the mixture is too warm. You don't want to scramble the egg you're adding in the next step.

2. Stir in egg. Add flour, baking soda, cinnamon, ginger, cocoa, and salt.

3. Roll out dough on a lightly floured surface, about 1/4 inch thick. Cut into shapes or press into prepared molds. Bake on a parchment-lined cookie sheet, about 8 minutes.

Note: spray the measuring cup with oil and the honey will pour out easily. When adding flour, add a bit at a time. If the dough seems too stiff or crumbly, add a little water.

Gingerbread cake
Ciasto imbirowe

This gingerbread cake takes inspiration from my favorite version of pierniczki, filled with jam and marzipan and covered in chocolate. If you want to simplify things, skip the filling and ganache. You still have a beautiful, tasty cake.

Ingredients

1 cup honey (or golden syrup)

1 cup strong coffee

1 cup unsalted butter

1 1/2 teaspoon cinnamon

1 1/4 teaspoon ginger

1/2 teaspoon nutmeg

1/4 teaspoon cloves

3 eggs

1 cup brown sugar

3 teaspoons baking powder

3 3/4 cups all-purpose flour

1/4 cup cocoa

4 ounce tube marzipan

apricot or plum jam

1/2 cup heavy cream

5 ounces semi-sweet
   chocolate chips

Prep time: 30 minutes
Cook time: 45 minutes
Servings: 14 servings

Instructions

1. Preheat oven to 350° F. Combine honey, coffee, butter, and spices in a saucepan. Heat just enough to melt butter, remove from heat. Spray pans (9x5 loaf + 6 cupcakes) with baking spray (the one with flour works best).

2. Combine eggs and brown sugar, slowly add in the warm honey mixture with the mixer running. Add baking powder, flour, and cocoa, mix until well combined. Spoon the mixture into the prepared pans, the batter is very thick. Only fill half full if you're adding the jam and marzipan.

Optional: add a coil or thin slice of marzipan to the pan, top with jam avoiding the edges of the pan. Then top with remaining batter.

3. Bake about 30 minutes for cupcakes, 45 minutes for the loaf pan. You can test for doneness by pressing gently on the top of the cake, it should feel firm and spring back or a toothpick inserted in the top should come out clean.

4. Cool in the pans for 10 minutes, then carefully remove and cool completely on a wire rack

Optional: Heat the cream and chocolate (about 1 minute on 50% power in my microwave), stir until glossy and smooth. Let the ganache cool for a few minutes to about 100° F. Spoon ganache over the top of your cakes. If desired, color leftover marzipan for decoration.

Rhubarb crumb cake
Ciasto z rabarbarem i kruszonką

This is a wonderful coffee cake – lightly sweet and ever so tasty!

Ingredients

Filling:

4 stalks rhubarb (roughly 3 cups)

3/4 cup powdered sugar

1/4 cup flour

Crumb topping:

5 tablespoons butter, melted

2/3 cups light brown sugar

1/3 cup sugar

1/3 cup flour

1 teaspoon vanilla

pinch of salt

Cake:

3/4 cup sour cream

3 eggs

1 teaspoon vanilla

2 cups flour

3/4 cup sugar

1 teaspoon baking soda

1 teaspoon baking powder

pinch of salt

3/4 cup butter, room temp

2 cups nuts

3 tablespoons flour

Prep time: 25 minutes
Cook time: 50 minutes
Servings: 16 servings

Instructions

1. Preheat oven to 350° F. Prepare two 8-inch pans, grease with butter and line bottom with parchment paper.

2. Trim ends of rhubarb and slice into 1/2 inch pieces, toss with powdered sugar and 1/4 cup flour, set aside. The rhubarb will release juices while you prepare the other components.

3. To make the crumb topping, combine butter, brown sugar, 1/3 cup sugar, 1/3 cup flour, teaspoon vanilla, and a pinch of salt. Set aside.

4. Combine the sour cream, eggs, and 1 teaspoon vanilla. In another bowl, combine 2 cups flour, 3/4 cup sugar, baking soda, baking powder, and a pinch of salt. Work in butter and add wet ingredients. In a food processor, process nuts with 3 tablespoons flour until fine. Add to the cake batter, stirring until uniformly combined. Spread batter in prepared pans, top with rhubarb mixture, and crumble crumb topping over the rhubarb.

5. Bake 50 - 55 minutes (internal temp 210° F). Cool before serving.

Apple pie
Szarlotka

A quick and easy version of Poland's apple pie and it tastes even better the day after you bake it!

Ingredients

2 cups flour

1 cup sugar

3/4 teaspoon baking powder

9 tablespoons butter

1 egg

2 egg yolk

2 1/4 pounds Granny Smith apples, peeled, cored, and sliced

1/2 teaspoon cinnamon

1/2 cup raisins or dried cranberries (optional)

Prep time: 60 minutes
Cook time: 60 minutes
Servings: 12-16 servings

Instructions

1. Preheat oven to 350° F. Combine the flour, sugar, and baking powder. Cut in the butter (with a pastry blender, two knives, or rub into the flour with fingers) until it resembles coarse meal. Work in egg and egg yolk, the dough will be crumbly, cover and refrigerate for 30 minutes.

2. Reserve 1/3 of the crust; pat the remaining 2/3 into a 9-inch springform pan, covering the bottom and the sides. Toss the sliced apples in the cinnamon, add raisins or cranberries if you're using them. Add to the pan, piling them up. Crumble the remaining 1/3 crust and sprinkle over the apples.

3. Bake for about 50-60 minutes, until crust is lightly brown and the apples are tender. If it seems to be getting brown before the apples are tender, loosely tent with aluminum foil.

Ingredients

dough:

1 cup milk

4 teaspoons sugar

2 packets yeast

4 cups all-purpose flour

1 teaspoon salt

2 egg yolks

1/4 cup butter

1 teaspoon vanilla

filling:

2 cans Solo poppy seed filling
   OR 10 ounces poppy seeds

1/2 cup sugar

2 teaspoons butter

2 egg whites

3 tablespoons honey

1 cup raisins

1 egg

1 tablespoon oil

glaze (optional):

2 cups powdered sugar

1/4 cup milk

Prep time: 4 hours
Cook time: 35 minutes
Servings: 25-30 slices

Instructions

1. If not using Solo filling, cover the poppy seeds in boiling water and let sit for a few hours or overnight.

2. Heat the milk to 110° F, pour into a large bowl. Stir in the sugar and the yeast, let sit for 5 minutes. Stir in the flour, salt, egg yolk, butter, and vanilla, kneading by hand to work in all of the flour. Cover the bowl with a dish towel and let rise until doubled in size about 90 minutes.

3. While the dough rises, strain the water from the poppy seeds using a paper towel-lined colander. Grind the poppy seeds in a spice grinder or a food processor, you'll get the best results with a spice grinder, but you'll have to process in batches. Combine the ground poppy seeds with the sugar, butter, egg whites, honey, ground raisins (process in your spice grinder or food processor and almond extract.

4. Punch down the dough, and divide in two. Roll each piece into a 14 x 10-inch rectangle

5. Spread half of the poppy seed filling in each rectangle, avoiding the edges. Roll up (on the long side), pinching to seal the dough, tucking the end underneath and pinching to keep the filling from leaking out. Place the rolls on a parchment-lined baking sheet, seam side down. Cover with a dish towel and let rise 35-40 minutes.

6. Preheat over to 350° F. Brush with the egg beaten with oil, bake for 35 minutes. Cool. (Optional) stir milk into powdered sugar and pour/drizzle over the rolls. Cut into 1/2 inch slices.

Poppy seed roll
Makowiec

A soft yeast bread wrapped around a poppy seed filling. While I have made my own poppy seed filling, most often I use the canned Solo filling. To me, it's just as good and so much easier. This is very popular for Christmas, but don't save it for once a year. It's so tasty with a cup of tea.

Apple fritters
Słodkie placuszki z jabłkiem

A cinnamon-scented fritter with apple slices. Have them for dessert, for breakfast, for a fun supper.

Ingredients

2 cups flour

1 teaspoon baking powder

1 teaspoon cinnamon

1/4 cup sugar

2 eggs

1 cup milk

pinch of salt

3 apples, peeled, cored, and sliced

oil for frying

powdered sugar for sprinkling

Prep time: 10 minutes
Cook time: 50 minutes
Servings: 10-12 servings

Instructions

1. Combine the flour, baking powder, cinnamon, sugar, eggs, milk, and salt in a bowl using a mixer or wooden spoon. Add sliced apples and stir gently.

2. Heat oil, 1/2 inch deep, in a frying pan over medium-high heat. Spoon batter into the pan, spreading a bit with the back of the spoon, making fritters that are 3-4 inches across (you'll cook multiple batches) cooking both sides until golden brown.

3. Remove and drain on paper towels. Dust with powdered sugar.

Ingredients

3/8 cup chopped walnuts

3/4 cup raisins

1/4 cup chopped almonds

1/4 cup shortbread cookie crumbs

3 tablespoons heavy cream

1/3 cup powdered sugar

1 tablespoons butter

pinch salt

1 teaspoon almond extract

2 cans of crescent roll dough

For glaze and topping

1 tablespoon butter

1/3 cup powdered sugar

1/4 teaspoon vanilla

milk, enough to make a spreadable
 consistency, it won't take much

1/4 cup finely chopped peanuts

Prep time: 20 minutes
Cook time: 12 minutes
Servings: 16 servings

Instructions

1. Process the poppy seeds, walnuts, raisins, almonds, and cookie crumbs in a food processor until the texture is uniform and fine. Transfer to a small saucepan and add cream, powdered sugar, butter, and a pinch of salt. Cook over medium heat for about 5 minutes, stirring constantly. Remove from heat, stir in almond extract, cool.

2. Open crescent roll dough and separate into 16 triangles. Make a 1-inch cut into the short part of the triangle (the side where you'll begin rolling up the dough). Put the cooled filling into a pastry bag or a plastic sandwich bag, snip off the tip or corner to give you an opening that's about ½ inch across. Pipe the filling in a Y-shape along the dough.

3. Roll up the dough, giving a horseshoe shape to the roll. Bake at 375° F for about 12 minutes, cool. To make glaze combine powdered sugar, butter, vanilla, and milk. Spread the croissants with glaze and sprinkle with finely chopped peanuts.

St. Martin's croissants
Rogale świętomarcińskie

November 11 is Polish Independence Day. It's also St. Martin's Day. I guess you could say St. Martin is the patron saint of Poznań. The main street is named after him, and the city celebrates his feast day more than Independence Day.

Legend has it that long ago, a Poznań baker dreamed that St. Martin rode into town on his white horse and told the baker to prepare this special pastry and to give them to the poor, so he did. The croissants, now regulated by the European Union, are rather dear.

When I attended a St. Martin's Croissant workshop hosted by the City of Poznań and the Baker's Guild several years ago, I was told that on November 11, 60 tons of this historic pastry were consumed. More recently, I've seen estimates as high as 400 tons. The bakeries must work overtime for days to meet the demand.

When I told a Polish friend, who is quite the cook, that I'd made my own St. Martin's Croissants from scratch, she was shocked and said, "no one makes them, we all buy them!" I understand why! The proper croissant dough is very difficult to make in a home kitchen. I don't have the option to buy rogale świętomarcińskie at my home in the States, so I take a short cut and use the crescent roll dough that you can buy in a tube. While not identical, it does have the advantage of being fresher. If the bakeries are working for a week to bake the many tons of rogale, the one you buy isn't going to be straight from the oven like this one is!

Crepes with cheese filling
Naleśniki z serem

Thin pancakes filled with lightly sweetened farmer's cheese. Top with fruit or chocolate sauce. Delicious naleśniki of all kinds were favorites at Pancake Square, a diner akin to Waffle House.

Ingredients

crepes:

1/2 cup flour

1/2 cup milk

1/4 cup warm water

2 eggs

1/2 teaspoon salt

2 tablespoons melted butter

filling:

12 ounces farmer's cheese

2 ounces cream cheese

1 egg yolk

3 tablespoons sugar

2 tablespoons melted butter

1/2 teaspoon salt

zest of a lemon

Prep time: 70 minutes
Cook time: 15 minutes
Servings: 6 crepes

Instructions

1. To make the crepes, combine the flour, milk, water, eggs, and salt. Let the batter rest for an hour. Add the butter and a little water if too thick. Heat a pan over medium-high heat, brush with butter. Add a scant 1/4 cup of batter, tilting and shaking the pan to spread the batter into a circle approximately 8 inches in diameter. Just as the top of the batter begins to set, flip the crepe and cook the other side for about 15 seconds. Repeat until the batter is used up.

2. To make the filling, combine the cheeses, egg yolk, and sugar. Stir in butter, salt, and lemon zest.

3. To assemble, spoon a line of filling about 1 inch by 4 inches in each crepe. Fold the sides in and roll to wrap filling. Lightly brown filled crepes on both sides in butter. Top as desired.

Beverages | Napoje

If you're traveling in Poland, you'll have to seek out hydration. The practice of serving all restaurant customers a complimentary glass of water is uncommon. Most people will order a small bottle of mineral water, sparkling being the most common. The free refill is unknown. What you can be certain of is that your beverage whether commercial or homemade will be natural and delicious. I know you'll enjoy these soft drinks and liqueurs.

Tea | Herbata

Fruit punch | Kompot

Mulled wine | Grzane wino

Cherry vodka | Wiśniówka

Honey & spice vodka | Krupnik

Tea
Herbata

Poles love tea, and overwhelmingly, they love it hot. Tea is usally taken with lemon slices and sugar, but you can also do a bit more. Try adding one (or a combination) of the items below including jam. Yes, jam! It will be the best fruit tea you've ever had.

Ingredients

4 teaspoons loose leaf tea

32 ounces boiling water

optional:

mint

lemon balm

dried apple peel

raspberries

dried rosehips

grated ginger

jam

Prep time: 2 minutes
Cook time: 5 minutes
Servings: 4 servings

Instructions

1. Add the loose tea to a pot, pour boiling water over the top. If you like, add 4 teaspoons of one of the optional ingredients: mint, lemon balm, apple peel, raspberries, rosehips, ginger, or jam.

2. Steep for 3-5 minutes. Pour through a strainer into teacups.

Fruit punch
Kompot

Try this fruity, refresing summer drink. Made from stewed fresh fruit and half the sugar in soda.

Ingredients

1 gallon water

1 cup sugar

10 dried apricots

1 apple, cored and sliced

6 ounces raspberries

6 ounces blueberries, muddled

Prep time: 15 minutes
Cook time: 20 minutes
Servings: 16servings

Instructions

1. Add the sugar to the water in a large pan. Bring to a boil, stirring until the sugar dissolves.

2. Add apricots and apple. Simmer for 15 minutes. Add berries. Return to boil and remove from heat. Cool.

Note: the fruit isn't strained out. It's common to have a few pieces in your glass.

Mulled wine
Grzane wino

A wonderful warm drink that makes the whole house smell good.

Ingredients

1 bottle red wine

1 bottle water

2 sticks cinnamon

3 whole cloves

1/2 lemon, sliced

10 teaspoons granulated sugar

Prep time: 10 minutes
Cook time: 1 hour 30 minutes
Servings: 6-8 servings

Instructions

1. Combine ingredients in a large saucepan and barely simmer for 90 minutes.

2. Serve hot

Cherry vodka
Wiśniówka

Homemade cherry-infused vodka. If you make this when cherries are in season (June and July), it will be perfect in time for the holidays. It will become an annual tradition.

Ingredients

2 1/4 pounds pitted cherries

1/2 cup sugar

1 liter vodka

Prep time: 1 hour
Cook time: 3-4 months steeping
Servings: 30 servings

Instructions

1. Combine all of the ingredients in sterile containers. Submerge the jar(s) in boiling water for 10 minutes or run through the dishwasher cycle with heat dry to sterilize.

2. Shake or swirl daily until the sugar has dissolved, it takes a few days. Store the containers (in pantry or basement) for 4 to 6 weeks. Strain and re-bottle. Allow to age 2 to 4 months.

Note: it's traditional to use sour cherries, but personally, I don't notice a difference in the finished product based on the variety of cherry.

 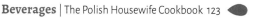

Honey & spice vodka
Krupnik

A honey and spice liqueur recipe that dates back 400 years. It's reputed to be good for what ails you.

Ingredients

2 cups clover honey

2 whole cloves

1 cinnamon stick

zest of 1/2 lemon, removed
  in strips with a vegetable peeler

1/4 vanilla bean pod, sliced open

1 allspice berry

2 cups vodka

Prep time: 15 minutes
Cook time: 15 minutes (2 hours passive)
Servings: 30 servings

Instructions

1. Pour honey into a saucepan. Add cloves, cinnamon, lemon zest, vanilla, and allspice. Warm just enough to thin (keeping under a boil) and steep on low heat for 10 minutes.

2. Remove from heat. Add vodka, and let steep for a couple of hours. Pour through a strainer, and pour into bottles. Seal bottles.

3. Serve warm, at room temp, or chilled.

Sponsors

Sincere thanks to my sponsors. These businesses share our love of Polish cuisine and preserving family traditions. They have made The Polish Housewife Cookbook a reality by covering many of the up-front costs involved in self-publishing. Thanks for supporting them as well.

Poland Culinary Vacations

- Small group tours through various regions of Poland featuring food, wine, spa, and cultural tours
- Hands-on cooking lessons in villages and urban restaurants
- Refined luxury hotel accommodations
- Visit us online at PolandCulinaryVacations.com
- Call toll-free 888 703-8130 (in the U.S. & Canada)

Polish Shirt Store

- The premier source for unique Polish-American t-shirts, Polish flags, and more. as we honor our ancestral past and show love to the fatherland
- Perfect to wear to a polka music event or Polish festival
- We carry Polish-themed gifts for all occasions
- Visit us online at PolishShirtStore.com

Acknowledgements

Heather Revanna – proofreader/editor

Heather and I connected on Facebook, and had a chance to meet in person recently. When this technical writer offered her skills on my cookbook, I knew it was in good hands. I've learned so much working with her. I'm grateful that Heather has also recruited her Polish friend Olimpia, who has been our final authority on the Polish language.

Heather has been a follower of the Polish Housewife blog since one day a few years ago when she needed a good łazanki recipe, and she has been hooked ever since! Heather lives in Denver, Colorado with her husband and son. These days she is a technical writer, but her love for Polish language and culture started when she lived in Krakow in the 90s.

Olimpia Kaczmarczyk-Benoit

Olimpia is a native of Southern Poland. She is an instructional designer and lives in Atlanta, Georgia with her husband and son. Living abroad makes her appreciate Polish cuisine even more and she works hard, with success, to pass her love of pierogi, naleniki and barszcz to her family.

Jeanine Colini – graphic designer

After seeing Jeanine's work on other projects, I knew Jeanine would create a professional look for my cookbook project. Her wealth of experience also helped me create a manageable process and workflow for this large project. I've learned so much working with her.

Jeanine is an award-winning graphic designer and internationally exhibited artist. She earned her BFA in communications design from Pratt Institute in Brooklyn, NY and moved to Los Angeles, California where she established Jeanine Colini Design Art (jcda.com) in 1986. She currently lives and works in Tucson, Arizona.

Sally Harris

Sally is my dear friend of many years who was kind enough to help me prepare some recipes and photograph in her beautiful kitchen.

Sally is the regional director for a youth-oriented non-profit organization and resides in Scottsdale, Arizona with her husband and their giant German Shepherd named Tate.

Index

P

peppers, 62
pickles, 11, 70, 87
pie, 105
pierogi, 43, 48, 51, 52, 55,
    56, 59
pierogi dough, 44, 47
poppy seeds, 106, 110
pork, 48, 62, 65, 66, 69, 70,
    73, 91
potatoes, 7, 38, 51, 76, 84, 92
Poznań 110
pretzel, 34

R

rhubarb, 102
rolls, 26, 33
Rosół, 8
rye, 19, 29, 30

S

salads, 79, 83, 84, 95
sauerkraut, 20, 55, 88
sauerkraut soup, 20
sausage, 73
side dishes, 75, 76, 79, 80,
    83, 84, 87, 88, 91, 92, 95
soups, 3, 4, 7, 8, 11, 12, 15, 16,
    19, 20, 23
Sour pickle soup, 11

Sour rye soup, 19
Spicy beet broth, 15
spinach, 52
sponsors, 126
St. Martin, 110
stew, 62, 65

T

tea, 116
tomato soup, 23
tomatoes, 23
tripe, 16
Tripe Soup, 16

V

vegetables, 52, 84
vegetarian, 12, 23, 52, 56, 59
vodka, 122, 125

W

wine, 120

Z

Zupa kalafiorowa, 12
Zupa ogórkowa, 11
Zupa pomidorowa, 23
Zupa ziemniaczana, 7
Żurek, 19

About the author

Cooking has always been something Lois Britton enjoyed. She grew up in a family that cooked meals from scratch. When she married Ed, an Air Force fighter pilot, his military career and moves around the globe exposed the couple to other cuisines and recipes their mothers had not made.

Finally, Ed's work took them to Poland, where immigration laws and lack of language skills kept Lois unemployed and asking herself, "Can an empty-nester be a stay-at-home mom?" Lois, a new food blogger at the time, made it her mission to learn all that she could about Polish food and the food-related traditions of family life and holidays. Over time, Lois' food blog began to focus solely on Polish recipes, and PolishHousewife.com has become a destination for Polonia around the world.

Lois has previously published an e-book, a guidebook to Berlin, which was near the couple's home in Poland. *The Polish Housewife Cookbook* is her first print publication and there are others in the works.

Lois and Ed enjoy spending time with their three adult daughters who are scattered around the western United States. Ellie and Rigby, two little rescue dogs, share the Britton home in Tucson, Arizona, where Lois, a certified public accountant, works for a large Episcopal church as their Director of Operations & Finance.